Home Staging Academy
presents ...

HOME STAGING SECRETS

FAQs

Answers to

Home Sellers'

Most Frequently Asked

Questions

by

Jillian Hinds-Williams
& Tina Jesson

Home Staging Academy
presents ...

HOME STAGING SECRETS

FAQs

Answers to Home Sellers' Most Frequently Asked Questions

Copyright © 2020 Jillian Hinds-Williams & Tina Jesson

First published worldwide in 2017
Updated in 2020

Published by: **Lioness Publishing**
LionessPublishing.com

ISBN-13: 978-0995069541
ISBN-10: 0995069549

About this Book

The Home Staging Academy, began life as a training division of Home Stagers, a nationwide business founded by Jillian Hinds-Williams and her business partner Tina Jesson. Home Stagers delivered home staging services for over 10 years before Jillian and Tina went on to build new successful enterprises, out of which the Home Staging Academy was born.

During their years delivering services direct to clients, they received hundreds of questions and calls for help and advice. Many of which are very much still valid today.

This book is a compilation of some of the most interesting questions, which they felt would be useful to homeowners, home sellers, home buyers, Real Estate agents and home stagers.

This is a very useful reference book for anyone who deals in real estate. If your client has asked your opinion or advice on a home related conundrum, chances are, you just might find the answers and suggestions they are looking for.

CONTENTS

Your Questions Answered

We got asked hundreds of home related questions each year - here are the top four
areas of concern

During our years delivering services direct to clients, we received hundreds of questions and calls for help and advice. Many of which are very much still valid today.

The key areas for concern were:

- Kitchens and Bathrooms

- Floors and Ceilings

- Extending a home

- Selling a home

This book is a compilation of some of the most interesting questions, which we felt would give valuable insight to homeowners, home sellers, home buyers Real Estate agents and home stagers.

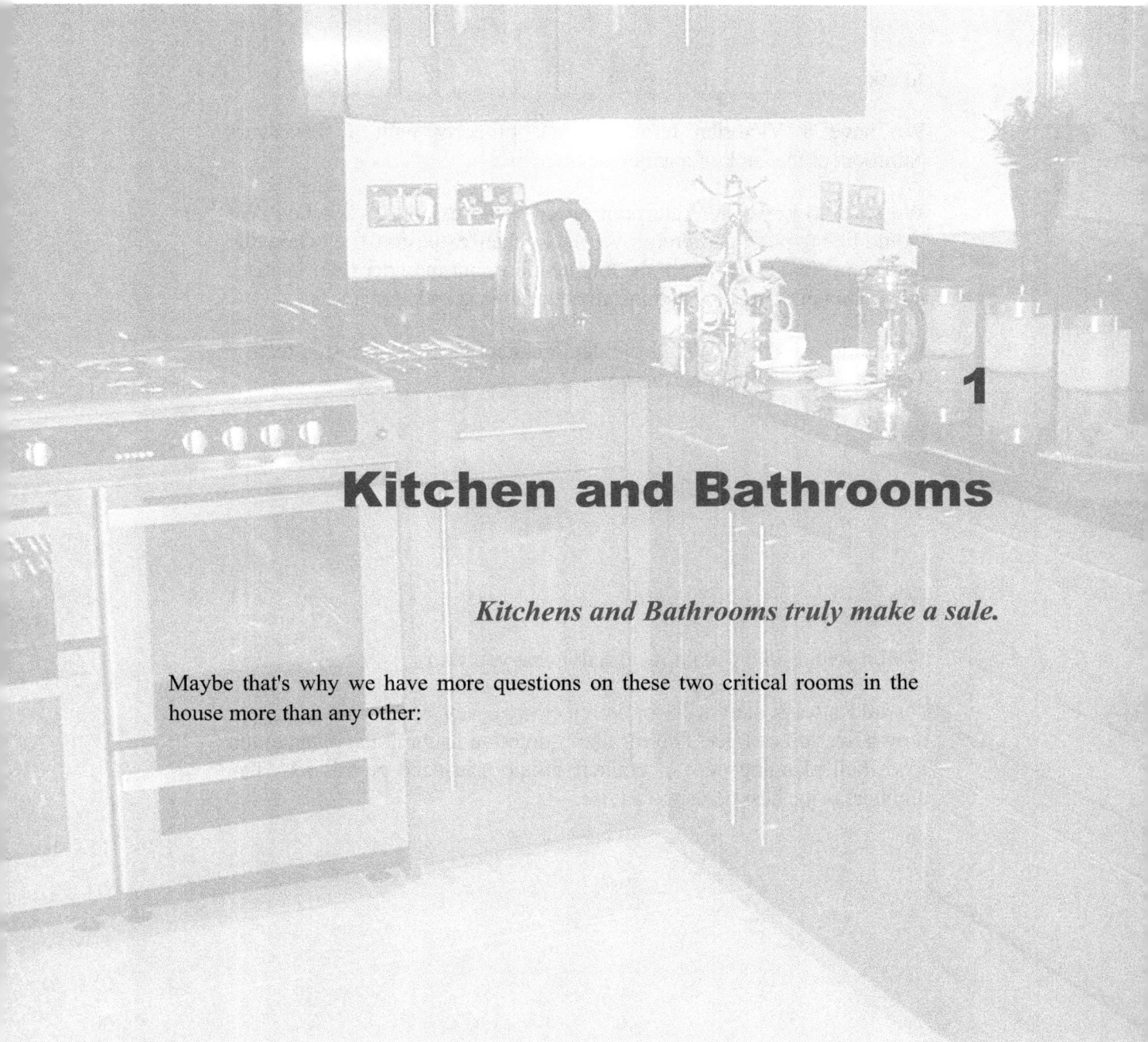

1

Kitchen and Bathrooms

Kitchens and Bathrooms truly make a sale.

Maybe that's why we have more questions on these two critical rooms in the house more than any other:

Kitchen renovations - where does Jo start?

Jo asked:

We have a Victorian terraced brick property with a downstairs bathroom at the back of a galley kitchen.

We want to move the bathroom upstairs and extend the kitchen. We would like to put a glass roof over the kitchen 'extension' (i.e. where the bathroom was) and remove the kitchen door, put in under floor heating, move the boiler upstairs and install new cabinets and appliances.

Where do we start ? With a builder, architect or kitchen design team ? Will we need planning permission.

Help !!

Our Advice

Hi Jo,

Well it sounds like you know exactly what you want.

I would always start with an architect, that way when your plans are drawn up, you can get "like for like" quotes and submit the plans to the town hall planning dept or council should you need permission. The architect is the best person to advise.

How can Michael lighten his cupboard doors?

Michael asked:

I would like to lighten the cupboard doors in my kitchen. They are currently in a dark oak stain and I am under the impression that I can remove this and lighten them by lime washing, can you advise?

Our Advice

Hello Michael,

Yes you can lighten them by "lime washing". You need to rub them down first with fine grade sandpaper to get a key and to remove the existing finish.

Then use a sugar soap - you can now get it in a spray. This is a great product to use before applying any wax, paint or a wash (which is just thinned downed emulsion) as it removes all the dust and grease from a surface. Then use paint on the lime wash. Work it in the same direction of the grain. You retain the feel of wood but with a much lighter effect.

Replace the knobs for a chrome alternative and it'll look like you've spent thousands on a new kitchen.

How can I promote the benefits of a small kitchen?

Brian, asked:

I've had my home on the market for a week now and we've had a few people to view. Unfortunately the kitchen is very small (8' x 6') and this seems to be the main negative comment on any feedback we have had from viewers.

We've been here for 12 years and haven't found it to be a problem other than when we have been cooking dinner for 6+ people. It is a semi-open plan into the dining room (which is 13' x 11') so when we've needed more work top space we've pulled the dining room table over to the kitchen and used that.

Any ideas on how to persuade viewers that it shouldn't be a problem when they come round other than waiting for somebody who's looking for a small kitchen?

Our Advice

Hi Brian,

Small kitchens can be a problem. I would suggest the following:

1. Clear ALL surfaces completely - leave only the kettle on display.

2. If you have dark flooring, replace it with a pale alternative.

3. Use a butcher's block for more work top space - not the kitchen table - don't mention that to your viewers either.

4. Make sure you have enough light coming in - clean windows, fit white roller blind AND turn on any under unit lighting - make sure all the bulbs work

5. If the work surfaces are in a dark colour, consider replacing with a lighter alternative.

6. If the unit doors are dark oak, consider using a lime wax to lighten.

7. Consider painting the open plan dining room the same neutral colour as the kitchen to make the kitchen area an extension of the dining room, and to make both look bigger.

Will opening up my galley kitchen affect the value of my condo?

Brenda asked:

I have recently bought a 2 bed condo and would like to make various improvements / changes, but want to be sure not to make changes that either decrease the value or make future resale harder.

The apartment has a good sized (for the city) reception room (4m x 4m). However, the kitchen is a long galley (4m x 1.8m) which runs the length of the reception room. I am debating the pros/cons of removing the partition wall (it is strictly partition) between the two rooms. I would include some form of breakfast bar as a partial divider between the rooms.

My worry is whether such a change will add / detract from the value when it comes to resale.

Our Advice

Hi Brenda,

As having a more open space would be more appealing, I would expect that you would make the space more saleable. Also by adding a breakfast bar, you would be adding a feature which doesn't exist at the moment.

Making profit on the modification will depend on a couple things though - like how much it costs to do and the state of the market when you come to sell. Providing you intend to stay put for a year - it is likely that you will get your money back, and make a profit too.

Our advice would be, if it improves the living space for you, do it. It will be appreciated by your buyers when you come to sell.

Is it worth replacing our yellow bathroom before we sell?

Brenda asked:

Is it worth replacing our bathroom?

We have a 3 bedroom brick terraced house, which we wish to sell. The bathroom is tiny and the suite is yellow, also badly lime scaled.

Although the rooms are freshly painted the tiles are ugly and will at the minimum need the grout freshening/bath re-sealing. Taking the tiles off will almost certainly mean re-plastering.

Should we bite on the bullet and have the whole room re-done (actually 2 rooms, as the lavatory is separate) or would it be more cost-effective to clean, clean, clean as much as possible, replace the carpets and then "dress" the bathroom as well as possible, leaving the replacement of the suite to a buyer?

I should add that my husband and I are both hopeless at DIY, and could do almost none of it ourselves, other than wield a paintbrush

Our Advice

I suppose the question is - do you want to make the most on your property as possible?

A new bathroom suite will certainly help you to get the full market value on the property and it doesn't have to cost a fortune.

You can get good white suites very cheaply from your hardware store - then you need the plumbing costs and tiling. Budget for fittings, suite, shower, tiles etc plus labour.

Don't be put off by the thought of replastering - you only need a rough coat to put new tiles on and the extra cost is marginal if you get someone in.

Getting the labour in might take a few months, so be aware of your timescales.

In our experience, the benefit can be as much as 5 to 1 - so think of spending up to £1,000 $1,000 €1,000 on a new bathroom to get around 5x back - £1,000 $1,000 €1,000.

If that's too much investment and time when all you want to do is sell then here's some quick tips to improve what you've got

- Use a tile primer and tile paint to make the tiles more up to date, seal around the bath and sink.
- Work with your yellow suite, use softer shades of yellow to complement what you have (never use contrasting colours). White and yellow look really clean.
- Buy a new shower curtain in white.
- Buy new towels
- Completely de-clutter all the bottles and personal items from the bathroom.

You still might find a problem, but it should stop people being completely put off or offering silly money.

How can John treat his pine cladding?

John asked:

Hi, I need some advice

I have just finished half panelling my bathroom in pine cladding, now I don't know what to treat the wood with.

Would I be better using varnish, oil, or a stain? I wanted to keep the natural pine colour. I've been told varnish will crack and make the wood go black.

Would oil protect the wood sufficiently?

I will still need to put a silicone seal around the bath, would it stick to oiled wood?

Any advice would be greatly appreciated.

Thanks
John

Our Advice

Hello John,

An interesting question. Cladding can be a good choice for a bathroom.

Using a wood stain should be fine as you are correct, varnish can get flaky in a bathroom.

You should have no problem with the silicon as that will adhere to your bath and tiles as well.

We had a cladded bath panel in our last property and it lasted a good few years.

How do I paint melamine kitchen units?

Claire asked:

I am selling my flat, and need to re-paint the kitchen units.

The cabinet doors are solid wood and painted white, the cabinets themselves are white melamine.

Please can you tell me how best to go about painting the melamine so it doesn't look obvious? I don't want a gloss finish as I think a chalky effect would blend better and hide imperfections that I am sure re-painting a kitchen will show up, so what paint is best for the doors?

I am sugar soaping the units and doors now ready to go so any help would be most appreciated.

Our Advice

Hi Claire,

Here are a couple of thoughts:

If you had unpainted wooden doors you could consider a lime wash, to give you that chalky look, but as they are painted white already I would suggest a silk finish. Choose a pale green or yellow and keep it quite neutral.

Depending on the type of update you are looking for, one idea would be to spay with a silver paint and varnish over. Another good tip is to use a textured 'Hammerite' paint - that would conceal any imperfections and you can get some good colour options - slate grey would look good if you keep the rest of the kitchen very light.

(Note: Hammerite is a textured metal paint available in Europe, South America, and Australasia. In North America look out for Krylon metal paint)

If you use a melamine primer - available at good hardware and DIY stores, to ensure a good 'fix' as your base, the sky really is the limit!

Add trendy replacement handles and you'll get that new look you've been wanting without blowing your budget.

Don't forget your tiles. Tile paint them if they wont match your new scheme and use a grouting pen to update the look of the grout. Other people's grime is such a turn off when you do come to sell, so don't forget to clean, clean, clean.

Will knocking 2 small rooms into one big one affect our home's value?

Lucy asked:

I live with my husband in a tiny 1 bed ground floor garden flat - a bog standard Edwardian conversion.

We share a front door and hall with the upstairs flat. 'Our' front door leads into a tiny, long, dark and very narrow hallway. Our kitchen (also small but lighter) runs parallel to the hall and we are considering knocking down the wall between them (not a load bearing wall) to open up the kitchen and make it big enough to eat in and light enough to like!

This would mean we'd walk straight from our shared hallway into our kitchen and lose 2 small rooms to make one larger, even though the hall doesn't really count as a room (it's so narrow we have to have 'passing spaces'!).

We can't bear it as it is, but want to sell up in a couple of years, so I'm wondering if doing this will devalue the property. i.e. two rooms no matter how small are always better than one. HELP!

Our Advice

If this is causing you so much grief we would suggest you do knock through even if it means losing the hall.

We would suggest that you can still keep a walk way though and the use of a breakfast bar - with the bottom blanked at the back (where your hall wall would have been - but not the entire length) could be a successful compromise.

At eye level you would see into the kitchen, but you would gain so much more light and space.

Use a light wood such as beech and laminate flooring throughout to open up the space.

Should I put in an expensive kitchen when I intend to sell in a couple of years time?

Alice asked:

We have just bought a flat that needs modernising and are about to put a new kitchen in.

With a view to selling in a couple of years time, should we put in a more expensive beech laminate kitchen or would white units be just as appealing to prospective buyers? (The latter being cheaper and our budget tight!)

Our Advice

Hi Alice,

My advice to you would be to look at "end-of-line" ranges from any national outlet, and go for a neutral modern finish. I would not recommend the all-white option - as it can look cheap and may need replacing after only a couple of years use.

We made-over a small kitchen with new end of line units costing a very modest sum, for a client with a limited budget, so it can be done.

Look at keeping the costs down by adding in a breakfast bar rather than fully fitted cupboards all the way around the floor space.

Using metallic (real or imitation) handles can be a cost-effective trick to keep the kitchen looking modern. If fashions change you can always change these.

Matching kitchen accessories can help too and you can take them with you when you move.

Will replacing my kitchen add value?

Mrs Williams asked:

I hope to move soon and am wondering if it would make financial sense and add to the value of my house for me to improve my kitchen before I try to sell.

It's in good condition but the kitchen cabinets and worktops are rather dated.

Would it cost a lot to replace the cabinet doors (the layout and interiors are fine) and the work surfaces with something more modern?

If so can you recommend any particular style/colour and where I might get them. Also, the two oblong metal grids that go over the top of the gas cooker have rather chipped enamel and are a bit rusty but so far I can't find anywhere to buy replacements.

Any ideas? Thanks in advance for any ideas.

Our Advice

Hello Mrs Williams

In short, yes. Improving and updating your kitchen can really help to sell your home. The kitchen and bathroom are considered by buyers to be the most expensive rooms to modify when moving into a new home, and if this looks like it will cost a lot for the buyer to do, it can break your sale.

While it won't necessarily 'increase' the value of the sale, NOT presenting it to best effect, may encourage potential buyers to submit lower offers, or make them reluctant to offer at all. This can make it harder to sell, and increase the stress of being on the market too long.

However, you don't need to spend a fortune on brand new top-of-the-range fittings to achieve an attractive looking kitchen that a new owner can live with for the first year or so.

At the very least, you should try to make the kitchen modern looking, ensure bright lighting, it must be de-cluttered, and clean, clean, clean.

We helped a client to achieve a totally new kitchen look and feel, which included a breakfast bar, new floor tiles and using tile paint to lighten the colour of the background tiles, all for less than his very small budget. We did this by using end of range offers from High Street suppliers. Although for that price he had to DIY the installation. But the effect was incredibly dramatic.

For another client we managed to modernise her kitchen, simply by replacing the cabinet doors, which was ideal as she too had good cabinet layout and interiors.

Try your local timber merchant for worktops, they do work out significantly cheaper than the High Street, sometimes half price, including delivery and cutting, and are of excellent quality.

You can get enamel paint from local hardware (DIY) store that works well for touching up chipped enamel

Regarding furniture hire, yes it would help enormously when you come to sell, if your property does have furniture.

American's have been doing this for years and it really does work.

However, this can be a costly option in the UK, as most rental company's charge for the cost of delivery and return which can sometimes cost more than the furniture rental itself.

Some companies also charge a minimum hire charge of 3 months rental.

However, rental companies that specialise in home staging, can supply furniture supplied with no additional delivery charge and rental periods as low as one month - just enough when you are looking to sell.

And of course don't forget that adding a few accessories can increase the aspirational effect, by adding a touch of opulence to your environment.

Should I replace the bathroom and kitchen before I sell?

Rosamund, from Sussex asked:

I am selling a one bedroomed flat in a sheltered accommodation block so I am aiming at a specific market - a buyer would have to be over 55 to live there. Prospective buyers so far have commented that the property is in need of modernisation. I thought that purchasers would prefer to put in their own kitchen and bathroom and so have left these as they are - they are both in reasonable condition. The flat could also benefit from a fresh coat of paint and having the carpets cleaned or possibly replaced. Do you think that would be adequate to give a better impression or should I have the bathroom and kitchen replaced as well? To add to my difficulty, I do not live in the UK and am trying to do everything from a distance!

Our Advice

Hi Rosamund,

It's true that kitchens and bathrooms can make or break a sale. It really does depend if you are looking to maximize your properties potential or are looking for a quick sale.

We would recommend that you do freshen up the decor with that coat of paint and do something with the carpets as this can be a real turn off to buyers.

We would also suggest that if your target buyer base is the over 55's, they are likely not to want to 'modernize' and would prefer to purchase sheltered accommodation that was ready to move in.

Bathrooms and kitchens don't have to cost the earth to update. Search out your local Professional Home Stager, and find one that specializes in cost effective makeovers on a budget. You can either project manage the job yourself, or if you don't want the hassle, then your home staging consultant can project manage the entire job for you.

I need a kitchen makeover on a tiny budget - HELP!

Michael asked:

This summer I'm putting my flat on the market, I have managed to decorate all the rooms apart from the rear kitchen diner which needs a good makeover. I have a very tiny budget- can you HELP!!

Our Advice

Don't panic, it can be done! In fact, we did a Kitchen makeover for under £500 ($900) that was featured in a national magazine.

For a kitchen, think: Bright. Clean. Neutral. Here's what to concentrate on:

Matching units that are well fitted (nothing worse than the viewer opening a cupboard to find the handle comes off in their hand!). Replacing units need not be expensive. Try the high street DIY and hardware stores. Ask about end of line ranges or special offers. Keep the style simple and avoid dark wood. Painting the units yourself is an option but this really depends on what they are made of and doesn't always look as good as you hope for.

A clean floor. A brand new floor is a good investment. White with a regular pattern such as a diamond insert, tends to look very fresh.

Tiles are usually best in white. Just use a tile paint that can be purchased in your high street DIY store.

Clear the work surfaces and clean until everything sparkles! Only leave a few of the essentials out such as the kettle and some coordinating accessories. Add finishing touches of colour such as a bowl of fruit and a couple of healthy plants.

And finally.......As yours is a kitchen diner, be sure to define the dining space (even if it is small) with an appropriately sized table and chairs.

My kitchen needs a makeover - what do you suggest for a limited budget?

Mrs Williams asked:

My kitchen has an attractive light, wood-effect floor and quite plain, white units and work surfaces.

The tiles in the kitchen are in good condition but shiny grey and some of them have fruit and vegetable pictures on them. They have to go!

What do you suggest for a limited budget and could you suggest a colour too, given that the walls are terracotta? I could change the colour of the walls if necessary.

Our Advice

Hello Mrs Williams

We would suggest that you use tile primer to paint out the grey. Then it's up to you on the colour. We would always recommend painting tiles with white tile paint or gloss for anyone looking to sell. It looks the cleanest and would work with your other white areas.

This may be too white, however, if you're planning on staying.

You could try adding the same terracotta paint to random tiles (maybe painting the fruit and vegetable tiles?). Mediterranean blue is another good highlight colour to use which would complement your walls.

Alternatively, you could paint them all in a Mediterranean blue if you like bright colours. Bright blue and white always look such a good clean colour combination.

Hope this gives you some ideas - but remember, with all paint colours - if you don't like it - you can paint it out - so give it a try until you find the colour that works for you.

What is a cheap make over for my dark pine bathroom?

Chrissie asked:

Our bathroom is completely covered (ceiling as well!!) with dark pine tongue and groove (yuk! not my choice). What is a cheap alternative /makeover as we would like to move but not spend a fortune on re-tiling whole room.

Our Advice

Hi Chrissie

This is a common issue for many 1980's early 90's - style bathrooms, when honey pine was very popular. Today with more natural tones such as beech and lighter woods being fashionable this dates a room considerably.

An inexpensive makeover is rubbing down the wood to remove the varnish and using a "lime wax" to lighten and seal the wood, whilst retaining it's natural wood appeal.

However, this can be very time consuming as preparation is key.

- Use find grade sandpaper to run down the wood.

- Use a damp cloth to remove any dust.

- Once dry, apply lime wax with fine grade wire wool.

You can get lime wax from any DIY and hardware stores.

Get the idea - there are loads you can do with kitchens and bathrooms without spending a fortune.

On the subject of lime wax, we do get a number of questions like:

Do you know another name for Lime Wax in the U.S.?

Regina, from the U.S asked:

Hi, I'm hoping you can help me. I am very interested in a product called lime wax. However, here in the U.S., I can't find it.

I can't believe that it doesn't exist here. . .I suspect that it goes by a different name. Therein lies my question. . .do you know another name for lime wax? If so, would you be kind enough to supply me with that information? I'd be ever so grateful.

Thank you for your time. . . Regina

And...

Where can Eric find Lime Wax in South Africa?

Eric from South Africa asked:

I am unable to locate a supplier of Lime Wax in South Africa, can you help?

Thanks and regards, Eric.

Our Advice

Hi Regina & Eric,

In North America 'Lime Wax' is commonly known as 'Liming wax' - I have found one on-line supplier in the USA for you:

try: www.briwax-online.com/wax.html

2

Floors and Ceilings

These are notorious problem areas, especially in the realms of the inherited polystyrene ceiling tiles or dreaded Artex…

How can Danny finish his unsightly ceiling?

Danny asked:

I have recently fitted a new kitchen. in doing so I changed it from a partitioned kitchen and dining area to a large kitchen.

However this has left me with a very unsightly ceiling. the main problem is that it has been Artexed using two completely different styles, with a smooth band in the middle where the partition wall was. Obviously polystyrene tiles are no longer an alternative - so what are my options other then re-plastering or sanding. Is there an acceptable type of tile? Many thanks.

Our Advice

Hi Danny,

We've not come across an alternative tile. And can only think of a few of options:

1. Have the ceilings skimmed by a professional plasterer

2. Have a false ceiling fitted (more expensive than 1)

3. Clad with tongue and groove and wax to keep it light (not ideal and more expensive than 1)

4. Go on a plastering night class and learn to do it yourself

We think option 1, having it skimmed, would be the best choice though.

How can Donna fill a hole in her floor?

Donna asked:

How would I go about filling a hole which is just exposed concrete then applying my new lino to the area?

Our Advice

Hello Donna,

What you need to do is use a concrete mix to fill in - make sure any dust is removed from the area first. A self-levelling compound can be used on larger areas to level off the entire floor if required.

How can Helen fix her floor grout?

Helen asked:

Unfortunately I tried cleaning terracotta floor tiles with diluted caustic soda and the black grouting has now gone patchy grey - how can I blacken the grouting without having to regrout the whole area?

Our Advice

The black grout is due to years of build up over a long period of time.

Try using a permanent marker pen to fill in the greyer areas. If the grout is missing in places, try a grouting pen to replace the missing grout and then 'colour in'.

How can Dave cover his wooden ceiling?

Dave asked:

I have wooden ceilings downstairs, without removing them what can I do to cover them up?

Could I plaster over them?

Our Advice

Hi Dave,

When you say 'wooden' I am assuming you mean 'cladded' in wood. I also assume that the colour would be orange/honey pine?

Well you wanted options so here goes:

If you want to plaster you will need to board with plaster board first (We're assuming here that you have ridges in the 'cladding')

Rub down and wax to leave the look of the wood

Paint with satin finish to lighten but keep the wood

Remove them and skim with plaster

Is it difficult to get rid of Artex?

Lorraine asked:

Is it very difficult to get rid of Artex? What would the cost be approximately per square metre?

Thanks in advance

Our Advice

Hi Lorraine,

Unless the Artex is especially deep and really ugly, we wouldn't even think about removing it. You may be opening up a can of worms you didn't bargain for.

However, if you really can't live with it any more, then you should take into account the following before going ahead:

- If its thin Artex, then you will need to have the whole area re-plastered.

- If it's thick and you have it removed, it means having it sanded down - very dusty and time consuming.

- You also have be careful if the Artex is pre - 50's as some types do have asbestos in it and that could cost you thousands.

Our advice is, don't do anything until you have consulted a recommended plasterer to advise for your specific requirements, and they will give you a quote for the job.

Will laminate flooring put off buyers?

Julie, from Honiton asked:

Dear Tina

I live in a two-bedroom bungalow and intend moving in the next couple of years. I am considering replacing all the carpets with laminate flooring.

I expect most potential buyers for the property will be older people. Is laminate flooring likely to put them off?

Our Advice

Hi Julie,

Laminate flooring sounds like a good idea. Don't assume just because you live in a bungalow, that your buyers will be older people. Many younger people buy bungalows too.

Older people we have recommended it to have been very pleased with laminate and wood floors. As well as the aesthetics, they have also been pleased to find it easier to keep clean than carpet.

And don't forget the health benefits and dust reduction of a carpet free home.

You should ensure rugs have non-slip grippers to save you skidding around.

We think having good quality flooring throughout can only be a bonus. Make sure it is good quality though. Some laminate can start to split at the joints after a couple of years.

Can I paint my kitchen floor tiles?

John, from Basingstoke asked:

I want to change the colour of the diamond insert tiles in my kitchen floor - can I paint them or somehow replace them without the expense of taking up the whole kitchen floor?

Our Advice

You can try floor paint, which can work well, **providing** you do your preparation properly.

Before you start, use sugar soap to remove all traces of grease. Paint on at least two coats and seal with yacht varnish.

You can blank out the diamond shapes with low adhesive masking tape. Then keep the main colour and just paint in the diamond (or the other way around).

Yes this **is** a lot of work and in a much used room like a kitchen , can be unpractical.

Another alternative would be to use a cushion flooring on top!

When laying lino or floor boards - how do you cut around awkward edges ?

Michael, asked:

When laying lino or floor boards - how do you cut around awkward edges ? Can you provide a step by step guide?

Our Advice

Tiles and planks of laminate are much easier to lay than full 'off the roll' vinyl, but you can always use a cardboard template for the tricky areas. If you are not a DIY kind of person and the area you are covering is large, I would recommend that you pay that extra to get a professional in.

However, if you want to have a go yourself try the following tips.

When cutting into a skirting, lay the plank, vinyl or tile to be cut directly on to the floor. Press its edge against the skirting. Using a pencil or biro, mark the other edge of tile or plank.

Place the area to be cut on a scrap piece of board and, using a sharp knife pressed against a steel straight-edge, cut firmly through the tile. It will fit perfectly into the space left for it.

Awkward shapes around sink pedestals, door architrave's etc, are best overcome by first making a cardboard pattern of the precise shape and transferring this to the area of the plank, vinyl or tile.

Where there is a radiator pipe, cut a slit from the back edge to the pipe position and then cut a circle out for the pipe. When the plank, vinyl or tile is laid, the slit will not be visible.

Painting a Garage Floor - Can you help ?

Mary Ann asked:

I have a question. We have a dry garage floor. We have painted it twice and neither time has the paint stuck to the floor. We live in N.Y. state and they use road salt. We would like to know if there is a paint out there that will stick to the floor. We know that it will not last a long time, but we are now painting it once a year. And we do not drive on it for two days after it has been painted and we paint when it is warm and dry out.

Could you give us any advice?

Thank you, Mary Ann

Our Advice

Hi Mary Ann,

You can buy **concrete floor paint** that is very hard wearing.

Preparation is everything when it comes to painting!

We suggest that you make sure the surface is cleaned thoroughly prior to painting.

Use detergent and a wire brush to remove any oily residues.

Rinse and allow to dry.

We recommend that you use two coats of paint. Allow each to dry before applying the next.

Attic ceiling has 25 yr old white polystyrene tiles - Please advise

Annie, asked:

I've just taken over my parents old house, which is a Victorian brick terrace with a large attic room, that I intend to use as an office/study.

The problem is the ceiling, which has old white polystyrene tiles on it, which must have put up about 25 years ago. The tiles are looking decidedly weathered with grey and yellowing stains. Some of the tiles have disappeared.

I'm concerned that removing the tiles will cause two problems. One, we may lost valuable heat though the roof, and two, I'm not sure of the state of the original ceiling, which may look pretty awful.

My question is: is there anything you'd recommend to improve the ambience of the room - at the moment we have natural light source from a dorma window, and a bright strip light - while also replacing the thermal benefits of the tiles.

I intend to work from home, so would naturally like the room to be comfortable as well as attractive.

Cost is also an issue, so any cheapish options you can recommend would be appreciated.

Thanks for any advice you can give.

Our Advice

Hi Annie,

We definitely agree, you need to take down those tiles. They are a fire hazard too you know!

You will probably find that when you take them off they will leave behind a little of the glue. Use a wall paper scrapper to lift it of gently.

You could use a textured paint to cover minor imperfections, which is a cheap option.

You could try covering the surface with a think linen. This can have some good heat retention qualities. The cheapest way to do this is to add some 2 x 1 inch batons running the length of the room and using a staple gun, fix the cloth in place. You can get large dustsheets very cheaply, which look remarkably good!

You could use wooden tongue and groove again fixed on to batons. This is a slightly more expensive solution, but perhaps the best for heat retention. You could use a lime wash to keep the whole area as light as possible.

Laying lino on old floorboards?

Scott, asked:

I want to lay lino rather than carpet on my kitchen floor.

It is an old flat with floorboards. Is this a good enough surface to lay lino onto? or should I lay plywood first?

Our Advice

Hi Scott,

Good question.

If the boards are old they are more than likely to be uneven.

For the best results, use ply. Otherwise the boards can leave an impression in the lino.

That said, it can be done. But be aware it may not look as good over time.

3

When it comes to Extending

It's not just about looking after the space you already have, but what about extending upwards and outwards…

Here are our tops questions and answers for those extensions and loft conversions

Does Keith need planning permission?

Keith asked:

I am looking to build a new garage 18 feet in front of an existing. The new garage will not protrude further forward than the building line but will be 2m closer to a boundary fence. The new garage will be 1.8m from the fence once complete.

The garage will be the same height.

Do you feel I need planning permission?

Our Advice

Always check any kind of extension out with a qualified architect.

Depending on exactly where the garage will be positioned will determine whether you will need planning permission. Often extensions can be built without planning permission under what is known as permitted development. So it is worth checking out what the conditions of this clause are.

Some Local Planning Departments run 'surgeries' where you can visit a Duty Planning Officer to discuss an outline proposal and their possible response to a planning application.

Because these sessions are generally free to the public it is a good value way of tapping into expertise.

In addition, Planning Officers can also offer some useful tips and direction about the type of application that would be most likely to receive approval. This could save you time, money and effort if you need to have plans drawn up.

Check with your local Planning Department to see if they offer such a scheme or any other form of free advice.

Can you recommend a guide to loft conversions?

Mo asked:

I am thinking of converting my loft. Is there a website or book which will give me good advice and instruction so I can attempt some of the work myself?

Our Advice

Hi Mo,

You might find these books useful.

Attics: Your Guide to Planning and Remodelling - John Riha

A guide to evaluating the structural and design potential of roof space, covering both remodelling and decorating. It features technical information on subjects from ceiling height and stair access to skylights and fire escapes. Templates with graph paper are also included for planning purposes.

Attics: A Quick Guide (The Quick Guide Series) - Mark Feirer, Dave Dchiff (Editor)

This book takes you from step one (sizing up the project) through wiring, plumbing, stairs, walls, skylights, ceilings and sub-floors.

Which is better, an over the garage extension, or a loft conversion?

Christina asked:

What would be better, a bedroom and ensuite extended out the side of our house over the garage? But the width is around 92 inches and the length is 185 inches so basically a long narrow room.

Or would it be better to do the same but a loft conversion? This gives more of a square room.

Which is more cost effective and gives better return for value?

Our Advice

Hi Christina,

Sounds like the extension may be a bit slim and the proportion of the loft conversion would be better.

For both options you need to look at the access points - you must ensure room for a full staircase on the loft conversion, and access through existing rooms/corridor for the extension.

Extensions are generally the best option, although you may need to reinforce the garage if the foundations will only support a single level.

We would suggest you get in a buildings surveyor or architect to get some idea of feasibility and get drawings done. Then you can get quotes and decide from there.

Can you advise the best way forward for a loft conversion?

KP asked:

I have a semi-detached property and want a loft conversion.

Can you please advise me on the cost and the best way forward for this?

Our Advice

Hi KP,

We would suggest you contact a reputable builder and discuss the practical aspects. You need to ensure that you do have the room to do this properly or you could end up losing money on your investment.

You need to ensure you have good access for a full staircase if you intend using the conversion as a bedroom space.

You also need to check that the joists would be strong enough. Getting them strengthened adds to the cost.

Should I extend downstairs or add a bedroom in the loft?

Patrick, from Northampton asked:

Am I better to extend downstairs (adding a dining room and bigger sitting room) or extend into my loft (adding a bedroom plus en suite)?

Our Advice

Hello Patrick,

Adding an extra bedroom and en suite, if done correctly, can add a significant value to a property because you are adding to the number of actual rooms. You must make sure you have the room for a full staircase for this option to work.

Extending the downstairs as a single story extension has a couple of drawbacks. Flat roof extensions can make a property look unattractive. You could compromise the remaining grounds of the property.

My advice would be to only do what you actually need as a homeowner, with intentions of staying in the property for a period of time, rather than looking at the added value the extension would have.

I'm Planning improvements, which would you recommend that would have the greatest effect on value?

Dave H asked:

I'm looking to make some improvements to my 1935 3 bed semi. Which would you recommend to have the greatest effect on value;

- large kitchen,
- reasonable size kitchen + utility,
- or loft conversion to add a bedroom

I'd welcome your views/advice. Thanks. Dave

Our Advice

Hi Dave,

It depends on how much you want to spend, if you need the space or are looking to make money. Remember that you should limit the amount of work you do based on the location and the fact that it will always be a semi.

If you are thinking of selling, we would go for the larger kitchen and cost effective units. Don't spend too much on a new refurbished kitchen when you could spend a fraction of that again, if you plan to move, keep the style as simple and neutral as possible.

If your kitchen is particularly small an extension would be beneficial. Separate utilities can add a bit more value.

Adding a fourth bedroom will add the most. However, most people looking for 4 bedroom homes are looking for a detached too - so don't expect to make as much as a detached.

4

When it comes to Selling

We see many common problems when people come to sell...

Here are our tops questions and answers for those who are selling

We need to sell, and get the best price possible

Jeanie asked:

We need to sell our bungalow and move down market before retirement. Although we have a detached bungalow in a good area with a large garden and we are confident that the property will sell, we really need to achieve as much as possible.

We have 3 bedrooms. Two with fitted mirror wardrobes one with Artex walls, light coloured walls and skirting, light carpeting, dark wooden doors, one with sink.

During the 70s we attached beams to the lounge and kitchen ceilings. All the doors are wood stained medium oak with brass fittings as is the skirting board in the living areas.

The kitchen has American oak doors (honey coloured) built under double oven, tiled work tops, spot lights, vinyl flooring, white walls.

Should we put new flooring down? I was thinking of a light wooden floor.

Do you think we should do something about the Artex ceiling and beams? Should we leave the beams and Artex ceiling in the lounge? any suggestions?

I have two medium oak settees with beige covers an oak corner dresser. We have metal patio doors in the lounge.

The house is decorated in mostly neutral colours but I have a plain red carpet in the lounge hall and dining room. Would you replace this?

The dining room has a pine table chairs and dresser and beech wood settee.

My husband thinks it's a waste of money upgrading and we'd still sell without doing anything but I'm not sure if we would achieve as much.

I would very much appreciate your suggestions.

Our Advice

Your house sounds as if it could do with quite a bit of money spending on it to bring it up to date.

Dark wooden false beams are not in fashion as they were in the 1970's and the Artex will certainly put people off buying.

Keep the replacement carpet to a cost-effective option - go for a neutral Berber in light beige.

Go for a pale lino in the kitchen and take up any carpet you have in the bathroom too and replace with lino tiles.

We made over a house who had some of the same 'features' as you describe and they really did struggle to sell before they called in a professional home stager.

It sounds like you know exactly what needs doing and we hope you can persuade your hubby to take note.

Should I convert my extra kitchen back into a bedroom before I sell?

Martin asked:

I have a three bed brick terrace. I converted the smallest bedroom into a kitchen some years ago to rent out.

I'm now planning to sell. Do I leave the kitchen in? or do I return the property to its original three beds? I would appreciate your advice.

Our Advice

It really depends if you have converted the property into two discrete flats or not (with two bathrooms).

If you sell it as it stands, who would be your prospective buyer?

Would you only be targeting someone looking to 'buy to let' or to 'share'?

Is there a sitting tenant? This would limit your buyer base.

More bedrooms will return a higher valuation, as larger spaces are always more sought after.

If it's not two discrete flats, having a bedroom as a kitchen would look very 'odd' if it was left 'as is'. 'Odd' is a negative you need to remove.

Our advice would be to return the room to a bedroom before you put it on the market and push it toward people wanting to move out of one bedroom flats.

We are trying to sell our empty cottage, should we stage the rooms or leave empty?

Cheryl asked:

We have moved out of the cottage we are trying to sell.

It has no furniture only bits and pieces, like dried flowers and whicker baskets etc.

What can I do to make it look more attractive and cozy?

Is it better, in your opinion, to stage the rooms as if they are still lived in? or leave all rooms empty, so they look larger ?

Our Advice

Hi Cheryl,

This is a good question, which we got asked a lot.

What can you do to improve the presentation?

Well remove those dried flowers - we know it's a Feng Shui thing but it makes sense - dead flowers do not give a positive impression. They will remind the viewer that the house is empty. They also collect the dust, so at a minimum remove these.

Add a vase or two of paper/fabric flowers. There are some good choices from garden centers. Choose cream lilies with large green leaves for best effect and a touch of opulence.

It's often not practical to leave a property furnished, but try to ensure that the place is warm well before any viewers arrive (especially in winter months).

Make sure you leave a gilt-framed mirror over the mantle to keep a focal point to the room. If you have a couple of large candlesticks, use them to balance the mantle.

Leave potpourri and scented candles in staged places. This can add a welcoming smell rather than unwelcoming empty smell you can get.

Use Vanilla scent, as it is a rich odour, reminiscent of chocolate rather than any strong air freshener that can smell like you are masking something unpleasant.

Empty or staged? Well a staged room will 'win' over an empty one any day - you just have to think of those lovely staged show homes you see.

Hope this gives you some ideas on helping you sell. Good Luck!

Should we pay to make substantial repairs or put the house on the market at a reduced price?

Ms Showell asked:

My father has recently passed away and my mother would now like to sell their 1960s brick built detached family home.

The only problem is, that as my father was very ill the property has not been well maintained over recent years and is in quite a poor condition.

We think that there are a number of major and costly jobs that need doing, including the replacement of the garage roof and wall, and a large terrace in the garden, which needs extensive rebuilding, work.

I was wondering whether it is necessary for my mother to pay for all of these things to be repaired in order to sell the property or to put it on the market at a reduced price as is?

My parents' home is in a desirable location in the city and the houses in the area command quite high prices, but most of the neighboring houses are expensively maintained, we are not sure if this is a help or a hindrance?

Our Advice

Dear Ms Showell,

In times like these, when a sad loss has occurred, the additional stress of having to sell the family home can be overwhelming. And the priority is to minimise your mother's stress as much as possible.

As far as selling the property is concerned, you indicated that you know and appreciate that in its current condition it will not reach its full potential and that is fine.

It sounds as if the property is in a good location and there will always be a property developer that will seize the opportunity to make the necessary alterations and undertake the maintenance to achieve the market rate.

We suggest that you contact 3 local agents and look at the optimistic and realistic pricing they will give you.

Then we recommend you call in a couple of local builders to price out the work you think needs to be done.

Get written quotes.

Take the middle agent's valuation and subtract the value of the identified building works. This will help you to ensure the price isn't too low. You will need to decide how quickly you do want to sell and that will have a bearing on if you decide to do any of the works yourself, or do nothing and keep the price low.

If you do need to sell quickly, then at the very minimum call in a home staging consultant. A home stager is an impartial professional who can help your mother to declutter. Decluttering a lifetime of special treasures could be the starting point of packing for the eventual move.

In addition the home stager can help you to restyle the home to present the property, as it stands, in it's best possible light.

Even if you decide to do the full project before selling, the home stager can relieve you and your mother, of the burden of project managing and coordinating all the trades until the property is ready to be finally staged.

Ultimately, your mother's circumstances will dictate the way to go.

There is no right or wrong way, just the one that is right for you.

We hope the ideas we have given you help you to decide your way forward.

I want to sell my small flat in the city. It's currently in pretty awful condition - Should I do it up or sell as is?

Mark asked:

I want to sell my small flat in the city.

It's currently in a pretty awful condition, and if I were buying it, I think I'd want to gut it, re-plaster, re-wire and re-plumb.

Is the cost of doing this likely to be recovered by the increased price I would get, or would I be better off just selling it as is?

Our Advice

Hi Mark,

If you sell a property with that amount of work needed, you may end up 'giving' it way.

It's worth getting quotes for the work you think needs to be done.

Then get a valuation from 3 local real estate agents and ask them what it would be worth 'as is', and then its worth if all the work was done.

Our feeling would be that you would get your money back (and some) as we expect the area you are in is still buoyant, but you need to get a local view on it.

Make sure you have enough funds left to redecorate, add a power shower and do up the kitchen.

These areas really DO help you sell.

How do I get more viewers?

Chris, asked:

Our house has been on the market for 10 weeks now with a local agent but we have only had 2 viewings.

Any ideas how we can generate more interest?

The agent has advertised the property 4 times in the local press.

Our Advice

Chris,

In our experience, if you are not getting many viewings, it is because the price isn't meeting expectations, and/or the pictures are not doing the property justice.

There are 3 things you need to ensure are right to maximize the viewings for your house.

1. Price

Some agents give you a high valuation just to get your business (so beware)!

This needs to be right for your property type in your area.

Check prices of similar properties in your area.

2. Promotion

It's good to see that your agent has advertised your property 4 times.

Check the online listing too, as 90% of all buyers now do their research online. Buyers don't buy houses online, but they do eliminate them. If the pictures aren't appealing, or the property details aren't attractive, then the next house is only a click away.

Ensure that the pictures you get really show off your house to its full potential. If you don't like the pictures, get them to do them again, until you're happy!

Get the rooms staged before each photo session. Internal shots can help make your house really stand out.

3. Presentation

We all know first impressions count, so make sure you maximize your "drive-by desirability"!

Many viewers 'drive by' before committing themselves to a viewing. SO MAKE THE MOST OF IT!

Ensure the outside of your home is always looking it's best. Clear garbage. Repair gates, doors, fences, windows. Give the outside a lick of paint to freshen it up. Plant and maintain flowers and plants.

About the Authors

Jillian Hinds-Williams is founder of the Home Staging Academy, British Academy of Home Stagers, Home Stagers Network, and Home Stagers the UK's leading national home staging business, a business entrepreneur, property writer and editor.

Jillian has lived and worked in Germany, USA, Canada, and the UK, her background is with Blue Chip IT companies. She left the corporate world to establish a successful nationwide home staging franchise business in the UK, and developed an extensive program of training courses for home stagers, estate agents and property developers in how to present and market property successfully.

Jillian is an experienced writer, editor and trainer, and a Fellow of the Institute of Technical Communicators. Jillian moved from Essex County, Ontario, Canada and works from her home in Derbyshire, England.

Tina Jesson qualified in Professional Interior Design at the National Design Academy and holds diplomas in Business Information Studies and Project Management and is a qualified training practitioner with over 15 years business experience.

Tina has provided expert advice to many of the UK's favorite property TV programmers, including: Channel 4's 'Selling Houses'; 'Location, Location, Location'; 'Property Ladder'; 'Downsize Me'; and the BBC's 'Trading Up'.

Tina is also a popular public speaker and has provided expert advice on the UK's national and regional radio stations; presenting for the BBC at national Property and Home Show events; and a public speaker at "women into business" events and network events across the UK.

Tina now lives in Central Indiana, USA, and is a regular guest expert on IndyStyle TV.

Tina and Jillian both worked for a time in North America, USA and Canada, and they successfully adapted the concept of home staging for the British market, after researching the North American approach.

Tina had first hand experience of negative equity on a property she owned in the mid 90s and first started to explore interior design neutralization techniques in 1995, before first going to market with the concept in 1999.

Subsequently Tina and Jillian set up Home Stagers Ltd, and from there the Home Stagers Network was born.

The Home Stagers Network established itself as an organization of property experts in the marketing and sale of property, in cost effective interior design upgrades and property buying, to cater for the full home ownership life cycle and specializing in maximizing the potential a property has to offer.

Tina and Jillian wrote the first training courses for the British Academy of Home Stagers, which received national accreditation via the National Open College Network. Students from Europe, North America and as far afield as Australia came to study with the British Academy of Home Stagers which was delivered in the grounds of a luxury Victorian mansion. The training program was further developed as a distance learning course, and is now available internationally online through the Home Staging Academy (homestagingacademy.com).

Jillian and Tina authored many articles on the subject of property improvement for magazines and national newspapers, and blogged on the Home Stagers web site (which won the Golden Web Awards for two consecutive years and the Community Web Award). Home Stagers had strategic alliances with many independent real estate agents throughout the UK and Home Stagers' consultants were regularly represented at the National Association of Estate Agents conferences all across Britain.

About the Home Staging Academy

The Home Staging Academy began life as the training division of the Home Stagers Network and national franchise of home staging consultants. Training was originally delivered as a residential program, in the grounds of a luxury Victorian manor house, and students traveled from around the world to study the program.

However, not everyone could afford the time or money to attend the residential training program.

So the Home Staging Academy was specifically developed to deliver the International Home Staging program of courses direct to students around the world via an online platform, and to ensure it was accessible and affordable to all.

The wholly online **Home Staging Academy** gives you a thorough grounding in the Art of Professional Home Staging, that is accessible to you wherever and whenever you are in the world at any time of day or night.

The modular program can be completed when students have the time to focus, whether they want to fast track in 6 days, take 6 weeks, or take more than 6 months. The student sets their own pace.

All course modules are accessible from any device, from PC, Laptop, tablets and phones. Found out more at **HomeStagingAcademy.com.**

The **Art of Professional Home Staging** training programme, is a comprehensive Home Staging training programme, which includes course modules to teach you the all skills your need to become a professional home stager.

Course modules available now:

Learn to be a Professional Home Staging Stylist this free module introduces the concept of Home Staging and to the complete course **The Art of Professional Home Staging**. The full course is aimed at anyone interested in the art of home staging, and anyone wishing to understand the basic principles of staging a house for sale.

Colour Planning introduces you to the key principles of colour, and how it is applied when staging a home for sale. Understanding colour is a basic requirement for anyone considering professional home staging as a career or business.

Space & Feng Shui Principles introduces you to the key principles of space planning, and how you can define space to maximize its appeal when staging a home for sale. Understanding space management is a basic requirement for anyone considering professional home staging as a career or business.

Lighting introduces you to the key principles of lighting, and how it is applied when staging a home for sale. Understanding light is a basic requirement for anyone considering professional home staging as a career or business.

Decluttering introduces you decluttering and depersonalization of a home and how it is applied when staging a home for sale. A room cleared of clutter makes the room appear bigger, more relaxed and inviting, and more attractive to a buyer.

Accessorizing is the final step in the home staging process and is an essential skill for a professional home stager. Well-chosen accessories balance the room, define it's function, portray a lifestyle, and enhance a home's desirability. DESIRABLE HOUSES SELL!

Photography for Professional Home Stagers is a vital skill when building your home staging business. Being able to take great photographs of your work will help YOU to build a top quality portfolio, which is both a valuable record of your work, and a show piece for your talent.

Handling Client Consultations for is a vital module that looks at why client situations can be difficult and stressful, and how to handle them with tact and diplomacy.

Defining Home Staging Services helps you to define and package your home staging services so you can sell and deliver the service to your customers. As well as step by step walkthrough lectures, you have each service fully detailed as well as downloadable templates for each service that you can tailor and brand for your business.

First Steps to Business looks at the next steps you need to take to get your home staging business started, addressing the questions of how to turn your talent into a business, transitioning from being an employee to being a business owner, and how to find your ideal clients.

FREE 5 Day Video Course, revealing the secrets to building a successful Home Staging business. Do you have the "talent" to be a home stager? How can you tell? How to transition to become a full time home staging business owner. Do the stuff only you can do, and build a team to support you. Be clear about what business you are in. Define your niche. Decide what you will do, and what you won't do. Gain visibility for you and your business - to be successful, It's not "who you know", its "who knows YOU". + BONUS CONTENT

More from the Home Staging Academy:

Home Staging Secrets

The Psychology of
Home Staging

This is an ideal reference book if you want to learn WHY home staging for sale works and HOW to put it into practice.

We explore the concept of home staging, introduce the theories, and define 20 key psychologies that when applied really do work.

This is not a glossy picture book, but a reference book that is educational and jam packed with enlightening content that will help you learn why Home Staging works.

In 'the Psychology of Home Staging', you will learn the science behind the concept of home staging, and the practicality of just WHAT to do in order to achieve a successful sale.

A must read for anyone who deals in real estate:

- professional home stagers,
- property developers,
- real estate agents,
- home buyers,
- and homeowners.

Available in Paperback and Kindle editions from **Amazon**

For more information visit
LionessPublishing.com and **HomeStagingAcademy.com**

www.ingramcontent.com/pod-product-compliance
Lightning Source LLC
Chambersburg PA
CBHW051422200326
41520CB00023B/7331